Agué Oxú awuéleton ʃ... ~ g

Voz de las dos orillas

Voice of the Two Shores

The Collected Poems of
Agnès Agboton

flipped eye publishing
London

Voice of the Two Shores

Published by flipped eye publishing
All Rights Reserved

The poems in this edition were first translated by Agnès Agboton from Gun to Spanish and published in Spain in two volumes: Canciones del poblado y del exilio (2006) and Voz de las dos orillas (2009).

ISBN-13: 978-1-905233-74-8

This book is typeset in Book Antiqua and Palatino Linotype

Printed and bound in Great Britain.

This book has been selected to receive financial assistance from English PEN's "PEN Translates!" programme, supported by Arts Council England. English PEN exists to promote literature and our understanding of it, to uphold writers' freedoms around the world, to campaign against the persecution and imprisonment of writers for stating their views, and to promote the friendly cooperation of writers and the free exchange of ideas. www.englishpen.org

Supported using public funding by

ARTS COUNCIL ENGLAND

Agué Oxú awuélèton sin Ogbé

Voz de las dos orillas

Voice of the Two Shores

Agnès Agboton

translated from the Spanish by *Lawrence Schimel*
and from the Gun by *Agnès Agboton* with *Lawrence Schimel*

Sendas inesperadas que se abrieron hermosas nacidas de una sola semilla liberadora.
A mis cuatro Huanñinan: Violant-Iremi, mon petit bijou; Dídac, Axel, Manuel.
A Lawrence Schimel, por su empecinamiento, generosidad y estima.
A Zoraida de Torres Burgos y Maya García Vinuesa, mis amores siempre cuidadoras.
A todos los necesitados de Libertad.

Unexpected paths that opened, lovely and born from a single liberating seed.
To my four Huañinan: Violant-Iremi, mon petit bijou; Dídac; Axel; and Manuel.
To Lawrence Schimel, for his stubbornness, generosity, and esteem.
To Zoraida de Torres Burgos and Maya García Vinuesa,
my beloveds who always take care of me.
To all those in need of Freedom.

Contents | *Voice of the Two Shores*

BOOK TWO
Songs of the Village / Songs of Exile

Translator's Note

I was introduced to Agnès Agboton early in 2012 by a mutual friend, Zoraida de Torres Burgos, after Agnès was invited to represent Benin in the "Poetry Parnassus" celebration held at London's Southbank Centre in conjunction with the Olympics that year.

Agnès had been living in Spain for over thirty years by then, and wrote not just in her mother tongue, Gun, but also in Spanish and Catalan. All of her prose (which includes essays on African womanhood, books on African food and collections of African legends, among others) has been written directly in the latter two languages, of her adopted home; but she continues to write her poetry first in Gun, self-translating afterward into Spanish. There is no literary publishing scene in Benin in the Gun language, so she published two bilingual poetry volumes in Spain, Voz de las dos orillas and Canciones del poblado y del exilio, featuring both the Gun originals and her Spanish self-translations. I am particularly fascinated with reading and translating other writers who create in what I often jokingly call our lengua madrastra – our "stepmother tongue".

There are no direct literary translators from Gun to English, but I was happy to work with Agnès closely to produce English versions of her poems for Poetry Parnassus. I translated a handful of poems from the Spanish, from both collections, and then had long phone conversations with Agnès during which she'd read the original Gun versions, so I could hear how they sounded. Then I'd read my English translations, so she could hear how they sounded, and we'd tweak as necessary to try and juggle both the content and the musicality.

Over the years, some of these translations have later been published in journals such as Modern Poetry in Translation and anthologies such as Poems on the Edge of Extinction (edited by Chris McCabe) and New Daughters of Africa (edited by Margaret Busby).

Eventually, Agnès and I started to look for a publisher who might be willing to bring out the two books, individually or together in one volume, and especially to do so featuring not just the English translations but both the originals: Gun and Spanish.

We're grateful to Mitch Albert and the entire flipped eye crew for believing in this project from the beginning, and for sharing our vision.

We're also grateful to English PEN for supporting this project with a PEN Translates award. Beyond just the economic support, it was a welcome belief in, and validation of, this collaboration that's lasted a decade now, to bring Agnès's work to an English-reading audience.

While many negative things have happened over these past ten years (including bereavements, pandemics, depressions and the ravages of time on our ageing bodies), there have been many positive things as well. One of those positives, for us, is seeing this volume – which collects both of Agnès's published poetry collections – come to fruition at last and reach you, the readers.

Lawrence Schimel
Madrid, 2023

BOOK ONE

Voice of the Two Shores

1

… Godó étonlè e wua ñin zanklé ñɩnɔn
kpodo oxjó didó yòkpovúlèton…

Zaan enin …

1

… Fueron luego las noches sin sueño
y las palabras infantiles …

Ese instante …

1

… They were long, the sleepless nights
and the childish words …

That moment …

2

N'non flinwué Navi
—ojhun jhun tchétonnon,
oxhó démè baba tché wúkúnmè dó—.
N'non flinwué Navi
tó là adokon enin kpa
fidé nundidó huévi sisó té
bò sò djè égbé oxjó tohuélè
vosóto ñinñin alòlili tohué daiton nan mi.

«Nun é yé nan mè
uè yé non yi
—mon anon dó nanmi dai—
kpèvi huè
duhu huè
yiyí djin enan nyin
djè huè do nan
ñon zan».
N'non flinwué Navi
tó nunsisa axhjimè tenmè tohué dji.

«Avivi man dé mè
—mon anon dó nanmi dai—
yadjidji osu man dé mè
oxjó didò osu man dé mè
dagbé do dó
djin édo nan nyin.»

N'non flinwué Navi,
n'flin alòtohuélè,

axjua didó gbétohuélèton:
«Ñeñe», wuè anon yólomidó dai.

Bò egbé, kpodí xjóxjó hjuénu,
«Ñeñe», sòvò tó sisé oxjó tohuélè.

2

Te recuerdo Navi
—sangre de mi sangre,
morada en la que germinó mi padre—.
Te recuerdo Navi
junto al lejano fogón
donde crepita el pescado
y son hoy tus palabras
la antigua caricia.

«Lo que te dan
es lo que se acepta
—decías—
pequeño
o grande
sólo aceptarlo vale
y debes saber
cómo utilizarlo».

Te recuerdo Navi
en tu puesto del mercado.

No cabe aquí el llanto
—decías—
no cabe el sufrimiento
no caben tampoco las palabras
y todo sólo
puede ser benéfico».

Te recuerdo Navi,
recuerdo tus manos,

tu altiva voz chirriante:
«Ñeñe», me llamabas.

Y hoy, como antaño,
«Ñeñe» escucha tus palabras.

2

I remember you, Navi
(blood of my blood,
abode where my father grew).
I remember you, Navi,
beside the distant hearth
where the fish crackles
and your words today are
an ancient caress.

"What they give you
is what is accepted,"
you said,
"small or large,
only acceptance is valid
and you must know
how to use it."

I remember you, Navi,
in your market stall.

"There is no room here for wailing,"
you said,
"no room for suffering,
nor room for words,
and everything can
only be beneficial."

I remember you, Navi,
I remember your hands,

your proud squeaking voice:
Ñeñe, you called me.

And today, as long ago,
Ñeñe hears your words.

3

Nein n'ka na wuadó non juii
to alè mion zozo éhé dé bla katché
—hunkpamè vodun éninton dénon yí mi—
kpodo awúvivè détó fifion dó,
    kanñiñlan mè,
vègo tché.
N'dó axjua enin
—okpa obudahóton, sísiò tenmèton—,
n'dó axjua enin
bó nunkuntchélè dégò kpodo dasin kpo masó kpé ba.

3

Cómo permanecer quieta
en el enloquecido fulgor de mi vientre
—esa morada del dios que me alberga—
y el dolor que me oprime,
cruel,
la garganta.
Lanzo ese grito
—morada del espanto, temblor del espacio—,
lanzo ese grito
y no bastan ya mis ojos llenos de lágrimas.

3

How to remain still
in the maddened brilliance of my belly
(that abode of the god who hosts me)
and the pain that,
        cruelly,
crushes my throat.
I launch that shout
(abode of fright, tremble of space),
I launch that shout
and my eyes full of tears no longer suffice now.

4

Afonnun egbé ehé ohjué sien avivó
bò n'hjein dó adò tchémè nun sisió
nunkunmè tchitchi mèsusu tonlè.

Afonnun egbé ehé, eeinh, ohjué sien avivò
bò n'nan wua tuun atan, hjuédjaimè,
afín ogbé kplankplan lèton dé kó kú abè.

Tó zánmè, ena wua ñin, tchiovò djòjhon mimion ton.

4

A José Luis Jiménez-Frontín, en el recuerdo.

Es gélido el sol esta mañana
y llevo en las entrañas el temblor
de tantas miradas apagadas.

Es gélido, sí, el sol esta mañana
y escupiré, al atardecer,
las cenizas de tantas voces acalladas.

Será, por la noche, un sudario la brisa.

4

In memory of José Luis Jiménez-Frontín

The sun this morning is chilly
and I carry in my entrails the trembling
of so many smothered gazes.

It's chilly, yes, the sun this morning
and I shall spit out, at sunset,
the ashes of so many silenced voices.

The breeze will be, for the night, a shroud.

5

*¡Ete nun dindin mon!
...Tenmè abènonton ehé
kpodo abè obunonton ehé.*

Zaan enin ...

5

¡Ay la distancia!
... Ese espacio de silencio
y ese silencio de espanto.

Ese instante ...

5

¡Ay! the distance!
... That space of silence
and that silence of dread.

That moment ...

6

¿Etè wuè ka gba gbèlògbè
tó tchintchin ojhun tchémè
kpodo zinflu sin yèlomè kpo?

Axjuale kpodo awùvìvèlò wuu ñìn kun
amon vitri ojhunlòton
wua gba édé dó nan tègbè.

Bò egbé n'kpikpon zinflu sin yèlò ...
bò nun kikon yuyudé to nunkó,
voòvuun osintonlè,
gbigbò gbèmèton,
atinlà dé tó dodomè,
atindó dé tó djihuémè.

6

¿Qué se rompió aquel día
entre mi sangre
y la sombra obscura?

Fueron fértiles los gritos y el dolor
pero el cristal de la sangre
se rompió para siempre.

Y miro hoy la sombra obscura ...
y sonríe un brillo negro,
flor de las aguas,
palpitar del tiempo,
ramas en lo profundo,
raíces en el cielo.

6

What broke that day
between my blood
and the dark shadow?

They were fertile, the shouts and the pain,
but the glass of the blood
broke forever.

And today I watch the dark shadow ...
and smile a black shine,
flower of water,
touch of time,
branch in the depths,
roots in the sky.

7

Yozó xjomèfifa avivò kpeèvi hjuédjai lokpoton.
Abè wua djò.
Srò ofunfun wuagbè, zózó nunkunlinlon enin.
Srò ofunfun wuagbè, eeinh;
bò fifanun, fifa djidjló.
Abè wua djò. Abè wua djò.
Kpèsè..., kpèsè... didó mètchélèton,
nundidó akpaton enin, ládindin ton.
Bò srò ofunfun wuagbè,
kikón wuéwué tó titrlen mi dú.
Kléklézé enin, kléklézé enin ...
Kpèsè, didó mètchélèton.

¡Eviví!

7

La cálida ternura de un atardecer de otoño.
    Silencio.
Nace el estremecimiento, ese ardor ciego.
Nace el estremecimiento, sí;
y el calmo, plácido deseo.
    Silencio. Silencio.
Kpèsè ..., kpèsè... dicen los míos,
tan cerca ese rumor, tan lejos.
Y nace el estremecimiento,
me devora el fulgor blanco.
Esa luz, esa luz ...
Kpèsè, dicen los míos.

¡Eviví!

7

The warm tenderness of an autumn sunset.
 Silence.
A shiver is born, that blind ardour.
A shiver is born, yes;
and the calm, placid desire.
 Silence. Silence.
Kpèsè ... kpèsè ... my people say,
that sound so close, so far.
And the shiver is born,
the white radiance devours me.
That light that light ...
Kpèsè, my people say.

 Evivi!

8

¡Agóo, agóo …!
Mi djó alió nan ogbè
bò mi sè yi lá nan zinguindi
axhjimèton

¡Agóo, agóo …!
Annon tchélè masò sigan wa gbá sé
tó tchintchinmè axjua
nundjratò non lèeme.

¡Agóo, agóo …!
Hjuédénun abè kèdè nan wua djò
—dèdè mè—
mi nan djè zonin zinzònlò bèdó.

8

¡Agóo, agóo …!
Dejad paso a la vida
y alejaros del tumulto
del mercado.

¡Agóo, agóo …!
No florecerán mis pechos
en el estruendo
de los mercaderes.

¡Agóo, agóo …!
Sólo cuando nazca el silencio
—lentamente—
iniciaremos el camino.

8

Agóo, agóo …!
Let life pass
and draw away from the tumult
of the market.

Agóo, agóo …!
My breasts won't flourish
in the din
of the merchants.

Agóo, agóo …!
Only when silence is born
(slowly)
shall we begin the path.

9

Son oxhue tché sin ugu
n'tó sisé,
ozán éhemè,
nunkikó atinlòton.

Zaan enin ...

9

En mi balcón
escucho,
esta noche,
la risa del árbol.

Ese instante ...

9

On my balcony
I hear,
this night,
the tree's laughter.

That moment ...

10

Ni Agbo ton
gbò non bè.
Enin wuè ñín ojhun dé gbigbon jhunkán tchélèmè,
é kadein gbau dó tàlè dji,
é kadein gbau dó djòjhun uviròlon enin
dé tó avi flinflin ví to flétchélè nun.

Ni Agbo ton
gbò non bè.
Enin wuè ñín ojhun dé donmi do akpa nan mètchélè,
bó kasò wua dein domi dín,
boya to mangatinsa
dé hjein ayihundidá kplankplan tchélè kpon.

Ni Agbo ton
gbò non bè.
Nunkò enin uwuè adó nanmi, tò tché,
bò godó éton awua doxhiami aman
dé non wua dío alokpakpa tchélè dò vèvèdji.
Egbé n'wua tó sisé abètoé, tò tché,
tó zinguindin alió éhélè dji.

N'ka wua kplon nun, ¿asé?

10

Cuando el carnero aparece
se ocultan los corderos.
Esa es la sangre que corre por mis venas,
tan ajena a las cumbres,
tan ajena a ese viento helado
que solloza en las ventanas.

Cuando el carnero aparece
se ocultan los corderos.
Esa es la sangre que me une a los míos,
tan lejos ahora,
tal vez bajo el mango
que albergó tantos juegos.

Cuando el carnero aparece
se ocultan los corderos.
Este es el nombre que me diste, padre,
y me enseñaste luego las hojas
que me teñían de rojo las manos.
Escucho hoy tu silencio, padre,
en estas atronadoras calles.

He aprendido, ¿sabes?

10

When the ram appears,
the lambs hide.
That is the blood that runs through my veins,
so unlike the peaks,
so unlike the frozen wind
that sobs in the windows.

When the ram appears,
the lambs hide.
That is the blood that ties me to mine,
so distant now,
perhaps beneath the mango tree
that sheltered so many games.

When the ram appears,
the lambs hide.
This is the name you gave me, Father,
and you later showed me the leaves
that would stain my hands red.
Today I listen to your silence, Father,
in these deafening streets.

I have learned, did you know?

11

Gligli dèdè djòjhon mimion éninton,
kikissi aga délèton,
désokpotó wuéwué, ékpein nin ohjué só to sisío
bò nundingbò, nun flínflín enin
yozó, wóowó xjóxjó eninton
dé nondò wiwa djikun djidja ton.

11

El suave roce de esta brisa,
beso de unas cumbres,
blancas aún, aunque el sol renace
y la ausencia, esa nostalgia
del cálido, lejano harmatán
que anuncia la lluvia.

11

The gentle brush of this breeze,
kiss of some peaks,
still white, though the sun is reborn
and the absence, that nostalgia
for warmth, distant Harmattan
that announces the rain.

12

Tó diski mè, Casals kpodo tchélo étonkpo, tó nun dò,
hangbé lomilomi dé oku
òsu ma n'gan dó abè nan;
amon abè wua djò bò
—godó éton, godó éton—
asògohun wua to taédé déton kpodo
vivi nundidò azan xjóxjó tchélèton
¡yiyí kpodo guigò tegbèton enin!
Yozó kpodo avivò,
owuan dagbé kpodo owuan gningnlan,
kléklé kpodo zinflu …
¡Nunlokpo wuè ñín kpokplèkpo, nunlokpo wuè ñín
                                    /kpokplèkpo!

Xjomèfifa kpodo kanñinñlan kpo.

12

Suenan, en el disco, Casals y su chelo,
melodías que la muerte
no ha podido acallar;
pero nace el silencio y
—luego, luego—
puntea el balafón
los lejanos sabores de mis días de antaño
¡esa sempiterno ir y volver!
El calor y el frío,
el aroma y el hedor,
la luz y la obscuridad …
¡Todo es uno, todo es uno!

La ternura y la crueldad.

12

On the album, Casals and his cello play
melodies that death
has not been able to silence;
but the silence is born and
(later, later)
strikes the *balafon*,
the distant tastes of bygone days,
that eternal coming and going!
The heat and cold,
the scent and stench,
light and darkness ...
All is one, all is one!

Tenderness and cruelty.

13

Nunkikó
gba do alòmè nan hué
sin fifa matin.
Kpèsè … kpèsè …,
ekoé.

13

La risa
se ha quebrado en tus manos
una y otra vez.
Despacio … despacio …,
se ha reído de ti.

13

The laughter
has splintered in your hands,
time after time.
Slowly … slowly …
it has mocked you.

14

Egbé adó to nunkuntoélèmè
adanun didò djikunton.

Zaan enin …

14

Hay hoy en tus ojos
rumores de lluvia.

Ese instante …

14

There are, in your eyes today,
rumours of rain.

That moment …

15

N'tó ñein dé hjein dó té, din,
tó nunkon nunkponun mè
bódó tó dindin afódó alótuhuélè ton,
alió dédjilè, alòví tohuélè,
wua dangbon do yi wlasusu.

N'tó ñein dé hjein dó té, din,
tó nunkon nunkponun mè
bò n'ñuein dò,
tó abèmè,
ató ténon kponmi.

15

Me demoro, ahora,
ante el espejo
buscando la huella de tus manos,
las sendas que, tantas veces,
han recorrido tus dedos.

Me demoro, ahora,
ante el espejo
y sé que,
en silencio,
me esperas.

15

I linger, now,
before the mirror,
searching for the traces of your hands,
the paths that, so often,
your fingers have travelled.

I linger, now,
before the mirror
and I know that,
in silence,
you await me.

16

Adó eninlè dé lilè dó sún hunkpamè
kotó hjún hjún hjuèkpo
oxjó osu kpakpa nandó zé
gbé éton dó donun.

avunlè, kpodo adògbó tègbè yétonlèton,
lon hiédelè dógbé lan hiétonlèdji.

Azan dé ka nan wua bò adu hiétonlè
man nan wua kpé lan kplankplan eninlè.

Azan dé ka nan wua …
Xjomè tó fifyón mi
kukúwinyan dèxíxó éninton,
dédó nandjè tegbè mon.

16

Tiemblan ya las paredes
del tan seguro reducto
y apenas si la palabra
ha resonado aún.

Los perros, siempre ávidos,
se han lanzado sobre su presa.

Día llegará en que no bastarán sus colmillos
para tanta carne.

Día llegará …
Me oprime el corazón
esa tímida jaculatoria,
siempre en futuro.

16

The walls already tremble
in the secure stronghold,
and the word has barely
echoed yet.

The dogs, always eager,
have leapt onto their prey.

The day will come when their canines are not enough
for so much meat.

The day will come …
That shy spell
makes my heart ache,
always in the future tense.

17

Ojhun dé hjunmyón tin,
ojhun dé non hjun hjuézun tin.
        ¿Mènun wuè ka ñuein fidé énon xjlua édé dó?

Axjua dé non tron son nunflòmè tin
kpodo alò dé yé ma sin gandonan.
        ¿Mènun wuè ka ñuein nun dé hjein yé dóté?

17

Hay una sangre caliente,
hay una sangre que corre.
        ¿Quién sabe dónde se esconde?

Hay un grito a flor de los labios
y unos brazos sin cadenas.
        ¿Quién sabe qué los sujeta?

17

There is hot blood,
there is blood that flows.
　　　Who knows where it hides?

There is a shout on the tip of the lips
and some arms without chains.
　　　Who knows what anchors them?

18

¡Mi kpon!
yé tó zinguindin dó tó agbaza tchémè,
bótó nunkunmè huhuzú,
voo-dunlè.

¡Mi kpon!
Yé xhuélé mi kpo
alòlè zizéyi sò yi aga ...
nan mèdé yé man ñuein éninlè.
Agaaa, agaaa ...

¿Ogbò wuè yé ñin a?
¿Jalan wuè yé ñin a?
¿Avun wuè yé ñin a?

Mèdé ni sa djalé bo wua bòmi,
mèdé ni sa djalé bo wua sè yí,
agbaza tché titrlen kidja kidja non.

N'na sen oya tché nan yé,
juii juii mè,
avivi masò nan tó emè.
N'ma sò nagbè déhé din
nan katché sin kòhjuhjú.

18

¡Mirad!
Se debaten en mí,
furiosos,
los vodúns.

¡Mirad!
Me ofrecen
levantando brazos …
a esos desconocidos.
Arriba, arriba …

¿Son chivos?
¿Son cerdos?
¿Son perros?

Que alguien me eche ya una mano,
que alguien se acerque,
recoja mi cuerpo hecho un guiñapo.

Les consagré ya mi dolor,
silenciosa,
sin llanto.
No me negaré ya
a la sed de mis entrañas.

18

Look!
They debate within me,
enraged,
the *voduns*.

Look!
They offer me,
raising their hands
to those strangers.
Up, up ...

Are they goats?
Are they pigs?
Are they dogs?

Let someone give me a hand,
let someone approach,
gather my body turned into a wreck.

I shall now consecrate my pain to them,
in silence,
without cries.
I shall not deny now
the thirst of my belly.

19

Zán tó kuku
bò tó dètitènon sin zinflumè
djòjhon flinflin
matèsó tó ñinñin
flèflè.

Zaan enin ...

19

Anochece
y en la muda penumbra
ni siquiera
la brisa
sisea.

Ese instante ...

19

Night falls
and in the mute penumbra
not even
the breeze
hisses.

That moment …

Yé wua zé kon dó, nunkuntchémin,
nun fyon wu agbaza djidja gbètolèton,
alò iétonlè kpodo alòvi kiklin du iéton,
ota iétonlè dédí agunkèlè,
dé yé fèn kpodo ñyiñyon iéton. Cádiz.

Lalólè sin oxjó sò dé wuayiton
wua tó sisió tó alòtchélèmè
kpodo nunvivè alió mètchélèton.

Yé wua zé gba tó tagló tchémè
Sisienkan nun nundidé
oxju gbètò délèton, kpodo afinfí didé iétonlè,
dé non tó guigó gbèlèlè ayigba dé nún dai ojhun iéton;
yòdó winnyantonnon éninlè. Ruanda.

Lalólè sin oxjó sò dé wuayiton
wua tó sisió tó alòtchélèmè
kpodo nunvivè alió mètchélèton.

Yé wua zé dó gò dó túkan tchémè
adòví hjunhjun gbètòlèton,
ayigba dé bombalè lè glénan,
dògbó dé su hjon dó nun dó nunkunnan
kpodo wuangbè okutomèton. Kinshasa.

Lalólè sin oxjó sò dé wuayiton
wua tó sisió tó alòtchélèmè
kpodo nunvivè alió mètchélèton.

Yé wua zé gba dó otó tchélémè
gbigbó jhun ñinñlan avun nunkanmèlèton,
un'wua tó kpikpon alò mímlèndélè
kpodo oba tritri yuyu délè,
mèyu sin agbazalè dé yé xhjò dó ayigbadji. Ceuta.

... bò yé tó zinzin mí.

20

Han llenado, horrendos, mis ojos
los cuerpos mutilados,
las manos de corroídos dedos,
las cabezas como nueces de coco,
resquebrajadas y pútridas. Cádiz.

Tiemblan en mis manos
las engañosas palabras del ayer
y la doliente senda de los míos.

Han estallado en mi celebro
las yertas imágenes fotográficas
de huesos humanos, polvorientas,
poblando una tierra que bebió su sangre;
esas avergonzadas tumbas. Ruanda.

Tiemblan en mis manos
las engañosas palabras del ayer
y la doliente senda de los míos.

Me han llenado el corazón
los abiertos intestinos de los hombres,
la tierra arada por las bombas,
las fronteras cerradas a la esperanza
de repugnante imperio de la muerte. Kinshasa.

Tiemblan en mis manos
las engañosas palabras del ayer
y la doliente senda de los míos.

Han golpeado mis oídos
los salvajes aullidos de los perros,
he contemplado las manos pulidas
y las oscuras porras,
los negros cuerpos derribados. Ceuta.

… y me aplastan

20

They've filled, horrendous, my eyes:
the mutilated bodies,
the hands with corroded fingers,
the heads like coconuts,
cracked and rotting. Cádiz.

The deceitful words of yesterday
tremble in my hands,
and the painful path of my own.

They've exploded in my brain,
those stiff photographic images
of human bones, dusty,
populating a land that drank their blood;
those shameful tombs. Rwanda.

The deceitful words of yesterday
tremble in my hands,
and the painful path of my own.

They've overfilled my heart:
the men's open intestines,
the land ploughed by bombs,
the borders closed to hope
of the repugnant empire of death. Kinshasa.

The deceitful words of yesterday
tremble in my hands,
and the painful path of my own.

The savage howls of the dogs
have beaten my ears;
I've contemplated the polished hands
and the dark clubs,
the black bodies defeated. Ceuta.

… and they crush me.

21

Nku-nku-nku, nku-nku-nku...
dèdè, ulidèlè
bè alió zizonni iétonlè
bò, tó là, yé to té neinkpon
dògbó lò,
kòta lò,
Na Miton lò.

Nq-nq-nq, nq-nq-nq ...
titólò tó hjluhjlu
amon tó lèblanun sin nunglòmè
kòtale ma só tin gba.

Avò flinflin ajhúnton
wua gblé oxhó kundidónon
nan Na Miton lò.

21

Chis-chas, chis-chas ...
lentas, las hormigas
inician su camino
y, más allá, les aguarda
la gran gruta,
la termitera,
la Madre Tierra.

Tris-tras, tris-tras ...
se agita la hilera
pero en las tristes esquinas
ya no hay termiteras.

Un velo de niebla
mancilla el vientre fértil
de la Madre Tierra.

21

Click-clack, click-clack …
slowly, the ants
commence their walk
and, further on, awaiting them,
the great crevice,
the termite mound,
Mother Earth.

Tris-tras, tris-tras …
the thread shakes
but now there are no termite mounds
in the sad corners.

A veil of fog
stains the fertile belly
of Mother Earth.

22

¡Xjó didòlè kedè,
xjó didòlè kedè …!
bò n'didin dodjrè enin
dé nan dó abè nan yé.

Zaan enin …

22

¡Sólo palabras,
sólo palabras …!
Y busco ese gesto
que las acalle.

Ese instante …

22

Just words,
just words …!
And I search for that gesture
that silences them.

That moment …

23

Bò hjuédjahi gbigblòló enin wua xhè nunkunmè nanmi
hjuénun annontchélè, do djèmein tintan tintan,
bodó ñin wuan flinflin nan alótuélè.

Bò kikon zinflúton wua xhè nunkunmè nanmi
hjuénun alótchélè wuató didó gansisé nunkan,
enin dé da amlon dó akonun tohué dji.

Kaka djè din xjomèfifalò sòtó kikon tó nunkunmè nanmi,
owuan nunnun flinflin yozó miton ton
kpò miton non.

23

Y me sube a los ojos aquella tibia tarde
cuando mis senos, por primera vez desnudos,
fueron el perfume de tus manos.

Y me sube a los ojos el fulgor de la penumbra
que mis manos sembraban en tu pecho,
la cadencia de aquella sabana adormecida.

Todavía titila en mis ojos la ternura,
el aroma de nuestra calidez
conjunta.

23

Into my eyes rises that warm afternoon
when my breasts, naked for the first time,
were the perfume of your hands.

Into my eyes rises the glimmer of the penumbra
my hands sowed your chest,
the rhythm of that sleeping savannah.

Tenderness still sparkles in my eyes,
the scent of our joint
warmth.

24

Ayó;
ohué zózó dúdúnon
kpodo oxjè kukunon.

Ohué zózó dúdúnon,
yiyí kpodo guigó dé mi gba
kaka dósó yi nan tègbè.

Oxjè kukunon,
wua djahi tò nègi
dé lilè dó nunkan yuyulò.

Ayó
—avòzanton kpodo ofúnlè—;
ohué zózó dúdúnon
kpodo oxjè kukunon.

24

Sexo;
una danza ardiente
y un pájaro muerto.

Una danza ardiente,
vaivén que construimos
eternamente.

El pájaro muerto,
caído entre la nieve
que rodea el bosque negro.

Sexo
—sábanas y pelos—;
una danza ardiente
y un pájaro muerto.

24

Sex;
a burning dance
and a dead bird.

A burning dance,
a to-and-fro we construct
eternally.

The dead bird,
fallen into the snow
that surrounds the black forest.

Sex
(sheets and hairs);
a burning dance
and a dead bird.

25

*Adó djidjrè alòtohuélèton
tó tchintchinmè anontchélèmè.
¡Etèe adan ohuédudú
ayó mitonlèton nien a!*

25

Tienes las manos medidas
en la línea de mis pechos
¡Ay qué danzas violentas
nuestros sexos!

25

Your hands are measured
against the line of my breasts.
Oh what violent dances,
our sexes!

26

¡Gbigbò sisien ehé
dé wua sin añin tó adòmè nanmi!

Nunlèkpo tó huédu tó ahututchédji
nunlèkpo tó huédu tó agbazatchémè
bó koxó ma só wua ségan
nan akeé fifiè okatchétonnon.

Voovun yuyu uwuè yé ñin dai
bò ohuélò ma sòdjè.
¿Mon wuè alòlili gbèton ton ñin dai a?

26

¡Esa respiración agreste
en mis entrañas!

Todo danza en mi piel
todo danza en mi cuerpo
y el ritmo exterior desacompasa
el grito adolorado de mi vientre.

Fueron negras flores
y la danza se extinguió.
¿Era esa la caricia de la vida?

26

That rough breathing
in my viscera!

Everything dances on my skin,
everything dances in my body
and the outer rhythm unbalances
my belly's painful scream.

They were black flowers
and the dance was quenched.
Was that the caress of life?

27

Djòjhon woówoton
kpodo sisiò nundjidjlóton:
alòlili lokplò wuè
non hjein —tó xhuégbé—
zózó myon.

Zaan enin ...

27

El viento del otoño
y el temblor del deseo:
una misma caricia
aviva —en el hogar—
la llama.

Ese instante ...

27

The wind of autumn
and the trembling of desire:
the same caress
quickens (at the hearth)
the flame.

That moment ...

28

Dasín abènonton
tó hjuédjai mè ...
Awúvivè djikun flinflin eninton
dé madindin nan ken.

    Tenmè matin nan ñein
    tó nun wiwua yéton
    hjuémètonmè.

28

Lágrimas de silencio
en el atardecer ...
Esa incesante llovizna
de dolor.

    No hay lugar para mí
    en las ceremonias
    del mediodía.

28

Tears of silence
in the afternoon …
That incessant drizzle
of pain.

> There is no room for me
> in the midday
> ceremonies.

29

Adóxjò là éninton
hunxjò hublanun tchéton nonlè,
bibèten nunkikó tché kpodo avivi tchéton nonlè.

Adóxjò là éninton
—dé ka wua sèkpo mi dó mon egbé—
démè n'dó gbè yokpovu tchémè dó,
démè n'yí owuan dagbé kunsinsen tchélè si
dévòsò tó gigò, kaka djè din, alòkpa nan mi.

     Nin sa djalé bó ñin, nan mi din,
     fifa tó ayigba dji.
     Bò ayigba énin nin sa djalé dó ñin
     yohó Ahwangbó ton
     dé nontó té non kponmi.

29

Esa lejana choza
albergue de mis tristezas,
refugio de las risas y las lágrimas.

Esa lejana choza
— tan cerca hoy —
en la que sembré mi infancia,
en la que recogí los olorosos frutos
que llenan, aún, mis manos.

     Séame pues, ahora,
     apacible la tierra.
     Y séame esa tierra
     el yohó que en Ahwangbó
     me aguarda.

29

That distant hut,
shelter of my sadnesses,
refuge from the laughter and the tears.

That distant hut
(so close now)
in which I sowed my childhood,
in which I reaped the redolent fruits
that yet fill my hands.

> May the Earth now be
> peaceful for me.
> And may that land be
> the *yohó* that in Ahwangbó
> awaits me.

30

Nake sin wuan nunnun
détó djidji tó xhuégbé
kpodo yozó détó amlonsisa dó nanmi
hjuénun avivó hongbodjiton
to drokù kpodo owuan ñinñlan ahimèton
wuan nunnun Adjarraton.

Yozó enin détó amlonsisa dó nanmi
kpodo wan nakéton détó djidji tó xhuégbé.

30

El olor de la leña
que arde en el hogar
y la calidez que me adormece
mientras el frío exterior
sueña los hedores del mercado
los perfumes de Adjarrá.

Esa calidez que me adormece
y el olor de la leña que arde en el hogar.

30

The smell of the firewood
burning in the hearth
and the warmth that lulls me
while the cold outside
dreams the reek of the perfume
market of Adjarrá.

That warmth that lulls me
and the scent of the firewood burning in the hearth.

31

Mèdé ma ñuein zonin
dé éozon dailè.
¿Etè utú yé dó nan nonkpon godó?

Éhéo, mèdé ma ñuein;
amon éyigbé nan dó djodó
dinló ohué daho dudu
bò nunlokpo dé wua kpo
wuè ñin nundé tó làyí.

Heviosó dó adan,
oxjó étonlè tó nun dó
bò nun dé masèten wua to titon.

Juii anan non, sa, non juii
ovitché,
gbigbò adòtchémè ton.
Masò sè tron tenmèdé blo,
asutché,
kun dotònnon to kò
xjomè tchéton.

Ñinsú kpakpá n'tó juiinon
(agbo biò dó mon,
agbo tó axjua éton keé).

Ñinsu kpakpá n'tó juiinon
nan mi ni dó bè, do okpò,
drudru dahólò.

31

Nadie sabe los caminos
que ha recorrido ya.
¿Para qué mirar atrás?

No, nadie lo sabe;
pero acepta ahora
abandonar la gran danza
y sólo permanece
lo que se aleja.

Restalla el trueno,
suenan sus palabras
y amanece lo inmóvil.

Permanece, pues, quieto
 hijo mío,
latido de mis entrañas.
No te muevas ya,
esposo,
sembrador en la tierra
de mi vientre.

También yo me aquieto
(el carnero lo quiere,
el carnero lo grita).

También yo me aquieto
e iniciamos, juntos,
el gran paseo.

31

No one knows the paths
I've already travelled.
Why look back?

No, no one knows;
but now accept
abandonment of the great dance,
and all that remains
is only what draws away.

Thunder rumbles;
their words resound
and the unmoving dawns.

Stay quiet, then,
my child,
beating of my insides.
Don't move yet,
husband,
sower in the land
of my belly.

I, too, calm myself
(the ram wants it,
the ram shouts it).

I, too, calm myself
and, together, we begin
the long journey.

32

Oxju lèkpo
tó nunkun énin lèmè
bò tó tòjhun xjóxjó lò dji
n'to déé kun.

Zaan enin ...

32

Todo el océano
está en esos ojos
y en la vieja piragua
navego.

Ese instante ...

32

The entire ocean
is in those eyes
and in the old canoe
I sail.

That moment ...

33

Djixuélè to gbigbó
bò gbètò eninlè
sò didó afó to komè ...
¡Heviosó!

33

Aúllan los cielos
y esos hombres
con los pies en el suelo ...
¡Heviosó!

33

The heavens howl
and those men
with their feet on the ground ...
Heviosó!

34

Ozán éhé dé gbigbè
akonnun éton nanmi,
ozán éhé wua to yiyò agò dudu
hublanun éton ton nan ñinlokpo.
Bò, un wua to minmon dèdè,
din nun wiwua tintan non,
ohué dudu dèdè naaxósi
Hogbonuntonlè.
¡Adjogán!
Amon, kpodo tasisien éton,
ozán éhé sòvòató gbigbè nanmi
osin amlon tché ton non.
Abè djan ekanan ñin.

34

Esta noche que me niega
su regazo,
esta noche me encomienda
el festín de su tristeza.
Y, despacio,
esbozo ahora el primer gesto,
la lenta danza de las princesas
de Hogbonu.
¡Adjogán!
Pero, terca,
esta noche me niega aún
el agua de mi sueño.
Silencio.

34

This night that denies me
its lap,
this night that entrusts me
with the banquet of its sadness.
And slowly,
I sketch now the first gesture,
the slow dance of the princesses
of Hogbonu.
Adjogán!
But, stuborrn,
this night still denies me
the water of my dream.
Silence.

35

Egbé nungblamèlè
to ñinñin dran gbèvihán odó wanton
nan avivò hjuédjaiton.

Gbètolè, yuyu, to wiwua
bo nontó owan obuton nun.
Yé dó to nunkun yétonlèmè
adukpikpa
kpodo agbò kpikpé ningbéton
dé obu yí.

Egbé nungblamèlè
to ñinñin dran gbèvihán odó wanton
nan avivò hjuédjaiton.

Yonsivi koklodjò awuédélè
wuató yiyi,
ogbé yétonlè ka wua nin
alió dé dein dó gbau dó tchélè
bodó wua titron son onun tchémè
kpodo nun sisió dé mon oxhó
lalo tonnon dé.

Egbé nungblamèlè
to aví axjuaton non vi
to avivò hjuédjaiton.

Vitrilè détó flétchénunlè,
azan godó azan
non wuató alió
alòtonlèmè súdomi.

Ohjon susu dótà nan gan xjixjolè
nonvè nanmi
kpodi akpa sin nun.

Egbé nungblamèlè
to handji
nan avivò hjuédjaiton.

Nan vò gó wua nan hué
bò hjuélonu osu, ningbétchélè,
nantó obu min.
Nan wua din tó akpa tohué
dòkpon adan nun
nundidó délèton
dé man ñin lalolè.

Bo boya djòjhon nan zéwua nanmí
vivèsin hjuèdjidjenon
nungblamèlèton kpo kpata non.

Egbé flétchélè to nun madó nunkununkpon
tché sin axjhua tchélè dó
nan avivò hjuédjaiton.

35

Hoy lanzan las esquinas
lamentos de cloaca
a la tarde fría.

Vienen, obscuros, los hombres
rezumando cobardía.
Hay en sus ojos
mordiscos
y un cansancio de espaldas
ateridas.

Hoy lanzan las esquinas
sus lamentos de cloaca
a la tarde fría.

Pasan dos muchachas
amarillas,
son sus voces unas sendas
tan lejanas a las mías
que rezuma de mi boca
un temblor preñado
de mentira.

Hoy lloran las esquinas
lágrimas sonoras
en la tarde fría.

Cristales en las ventanas,
cada día
me cierran el camino
de las manos.

Me duelen
las horas encerradas
como heridas.

Hoy cantan las esquinas
su desesperanza
a la tarde fría.

Volveré otra vez a ti
y estarán, también entonces,
mis espaldas ateridas.
Buscaré cerca de ti
el sabor arisco
de unas resonancias
no mentidas.

Y tal vez nos traiga el viento
el agrio gemido
de todas las esquinas.

Hoy gritan las ventanas
mi desesperanza
a la tarde fría.

35

Today the street corners throw
sewer laments
at the cold afternoon.

The men, dark, come
oozing cowardice.
They have biting
eyes
and the weariness of
numb backs.

Today the street corners throw
their sewer laments
at the cold afternoon.

Two yellow girls
pass by.
Their voices are paths
as distant as my own,
that a trembling imbued
with lies
spills from my mouth.

Today the street corners cry
noisy tears
in the cold afternoon.

Glass panes in the windows
close the route
of my hands
every day

The enclosed hours
hurt me
like wounds.

Today the street corners sing
their hopelessness
to the cold afternoon.

I will return again to you
and, then too, will
my back be numb.
I search near you
for the dry taste
of some resonances
without lies.

And perhaps the wind shall bring us
the bitter moan
of all the street corners.

Today the windows shout
my hopelessness
to the cold afternoon.

BOOK TWO

Songs of the Village / Songs of Exile

ALFA

Zan ehé, asutché,
zan ehé de man dindin, kaka djè din, nan su nunkun nan mi.
Zan ehé mè dé agbaza tohué bu do yi din
huénu, ato hjuii, toglò avò déchon huélè,
do non té kpon, boya kpodo gla kpo,
ogan dé nan drlanhué do ogbèmè
tò sò dé nan wa.

Zan ehé dé avunlè doyi gbigbó yétonlè do gò
bo dó gbon, huédélènu,
nundidò gadjan gadjan ohunlèton;
zan ehé huañinan tché nan wué
djè min dó avò dagbé dagbélèton mè,
djidjò vivi kpodo vivlonlè obu do wué,
e man mon ohó daho dahonon, boya tatanonlè,
boya lalonontonlè.

Zan ehé un yi hué kpodi nundé ma ñin kléklétché,
kaka do non djè gblòfifan dji;
kpodi nun dé yé dó nan wua, kpodo vivènun.
Vivènun dé ma dé yé ma dó nunkunun non xa nunkundji nanhué,
bonon wulu onunflòlè, wlasusu;
vivènun kpodi susu alòtohuélèton,
dé non lilè gòdó dó kpon mi,
bo dó non bió mi nun dé m'magan nan wué.
Vivènun kpodi nundé a dó nunkunun kpon,
yé man kan wuadjò,
kpodi alió susu nonlè
dé non tèn mi kpon,
kpodidò mi ñin nun tatadé
tó huedjahinun énin dé obu kpo nun ma donunkunun kpon
dó dó h'xjan adu do mi.

Zan ehé, wanñinnan tché, n'do nan sé wué djinhuè
gbon do sunu dé non gbon alòtohuémè tègbè.

98

ALFA

Esta noche, esposo,
esta noche que no quiere, todavía, cerrarme los párpados.
Esta noche en la que tu cuerpo se ha perdido ya
mientras, tranquila, arrebujado en la sábana,
espera, quizás con terror,
el timbre que habrá de lanzarte a la vida
mañana.

Esta noche que los perros pueblan de ladridos
y cruzan, de vez en cuando,
los rumores trepidantes de automóviles;
esta noche mi amor por ti
se ha desnudado de ropajes hermosos,
ha perdido exaltaciones y gozos,
no encuentra grandes palabras, tal vez inútiles,
tal vez falsas.

Esta noche te siento como algo opaco,
mío hasta el delirio;
como algo imprescindible y doloroso.
Doloroso en la desesperación que te sube a los ojos,
que te frunce los labios, tantas veces;
doloroso como tus puños cerrados,
vueltos hacía mí,
exigiendo algo que yo no puedo darte.
Doloroso como tus ilusiones
frustradas,
como los caminos cerrados
que nos tientan,
como el creernos inútiles
de aquella tarde en que el miedo y la desesperanza
nos mordían.

Esta noche, amor, te siento imprescindible
por la continua exigencia de tus manos.

ALPHA

This night, husband,
this night that still doesn't want to close my eyelids.
This night on which your body has already been lost
as (calm, wrapped in the sheet)
I await, perhaps with terror,
the doorbell that must launch you at life
tomorrow.

This night, which dogs populate with barks
and which is crossed, from time to time,
by the hectic sounds of automobiles;
this night my love for you
has undressed from its beautiful clothes,
has lost exaltations and pleasures,
finds no grand words – perhaps useless ones,
perhaps false ones.

This night I feel you as something opaque,
mine until delirium;
like something necessary and painful.
Painful in the desperation that rises to your eyes,
furrows your lips so many times;
painful like your closed fists,
turned toward me,
demanding something I cannot give you.
Painful like your frustrated
hopes,
like the closed paths
that tempt us,
like believing ourselves useless
of that afternoon on which fear and despair
bit us.

This night, love, I feel you to be essential
for the steady demands of your hands.

1

Filé, dé échikpodi
ganmè nonté.
Filé, dé yé djó ayigbadó
bódó yidó,
san avó tègbè
na onun linlin tata
kpodó ahuanganlè sin ohan kpo.
Filé, dé echikpodi
ohjun madó gbè.
Filé, to fifa
otètomè,
n'so wamon,
nun pkipkon sisiendé
nunkun gbigba délèton,
n'wa sé odhè
sinsin sin hodélè.
N'wamon ogbè pkèdé.

1

Aquí, donde el tiempo
parece haberse detenido.
Aquí, donde la tierra
es abandonada,
sacrificada cada día
a inútiles recuerdos
y a heroicos cantos.
Aquí, donde la sangre
parece infructífera.
Aquí, en la quietud
del cementerio,
he hallado todavía
la mirada fuerte
de unos ojos aplastados,
he escuchado las palabras
de una lengua agarrotada.
He entrevisto la vida.

1

Here, where time
seems to have stopped.
Here, where the land
is abandoned,
sacrificed daily
to useless memories
and heroic songs.
Here, where blood
seems fruitless.
Here, in the stillness
of the cemetery,
I've continued to find
the steady gaze
of crushed eyes,
I've listened to the words
of a stiffened tongue.
I've glimpsed life.

2

Edin, edin taun
avo yozoton
kpodo odin débió ayigbamè.

Edin, edin taun
Sèmè Podji sin agunkètinlè
kpodó ohjun dé hun alió.

Edin, edin taun
oko vèè dé yi mètchélè
bosónun, yohô sin sin, dèdè
hwuénué, afónnun tó fifa drótchélè
bó afòtchélè, tó sisa
dó ayigbanèlè dé kòmaxu

Fitèwè, fitèwè oko vèèlòté?
fitèwè, ohjun mèdjiton mitonlèté?
fitèwè, sodabi sisien vodoun mitonlèté?

Fitèwè, fitèwè oko vèèlòté?

2

Lejos, tan lejos ya
el manto cálido del viento
y el sudor que empapa la tierra.

Lejos, tan lejos ya
las palmeras de Semè Podji
y la sangre que abre caminos.

Lejos, tan lejos ya
la tierra roja que abraza a los míos
y bebe, despacio, el agua del «yohô»
mientras la mañana enfría mis sueños
y mis pies desnudos se arrastran
por esas baldosas sin sed.

¿Dónde, dónde está la tierra roja,
la sangre de las generaciones,
el ardiente «sodabi» de los dioses?

¿Dónde, dónde está la tierra roja?

2

Far away, so far now
the warm blanket of the wind
and the sweat that drenches the earth.

Far away, so far now
the palm trees of Sèmè-Kpodji
and the blood that opens the ways.

Far away, so far now
the red earth that embraces mine
and drinks, slowly, the water of the *yohô*
while the morning cools my dreams
and my bare feet drag
across those thirstless tiles.

Where, oh where is the red earth,
the blood of generations,
the burning *sodabi* of the gods?

Where, oh where is this red earth?

3

I

Nunkunctchélè dé madó awhu to dindin
tó calétalè sintòmè,
fidé nunkikolè pkapka
            non dió yédélè.
Agbaza tohué dé tó min
ka wadó avó dékpo huédévonuton a?
Hwuédélènoun, aló tóhuélèosu
            non dió yédélè a?

I

Mis ojos buscan desnudos
en el país de las máscaras,
donde incluso las sonrisas
            se disfrazan.
¿Hay en tu cuerpo desnudo
            restos de ropa lejana?
¿También, a veces, tus manos
            se disfrazan?

3

I

My eyes seek nudes
in the land of masks,
where even smiles
          disguise themselves.
Are there traces of foreign clothes
on your naked body?
Do your hands also, sometimes,
                disguise themselves?

II

Nunkuntohuélè dé to zèguè zèguè dji,
non tron nunkikomè bonon djè avivimè.

Yénon konu boku só nogó kpodo sin avivilon,
yénon viavi to tchintchinmè nunkikoton
bo énonpko tègbè tenmè
kpèvi
nan obuton.

Nunkuntohuélè dé to zèguè zèguè dji
non tron nunkikomè bonon djè avivimè;
yénon tron avivimè bonódjè nunkikomè
bo yénon hun yédé na obu.

Nunkuntohuélè dé to zèguè zèguè dji.
Vovuun yuyuu,
nunkiko kpodō avivi.

II

Tus ojos en el columpio,
van de la sonrisa al llanto.

Sonríen llenos de lágrimas,
lloran entre carcajadas
y siempre queda un pequeño
resquicio
para el espanto.

Tus ojos en el columpio
van de la sonrisa al llanto;
van del llanto a la sonrisa
y se abren al espanto.

Tus ojos en el columpio.
Flores negras,
risa y llanto.

II

Your eyes on the swing
shift from smiling to weeping.

They smile full of tears,
they cry among guffaws
and there's always a slight
fissure
for fright.

Your eyes on the swing
shift from smiling to weeping;
they move from weeping to smiling
and open themselves to fright.

Your eyes on the swing.
Black flowers,
laughter and lament.

4

Susu,
yentcho,
n'to chicho wiwa tohué
wihué.

A wua,
gan,
nunkun tohué dò nun
nun kpinkpen.

N'kpon hué,
nunkuntònon,
tata huè n'din homè
hunhuntoé.

Okpò,
minon,
bodó hó amlon bibo
miton.

4

Encerrada,
sola,
aguardando tu llegada
clara.

Has llegado,
duro,
en tus ojos hay un malhumor
pesado.

Te he mirado,
ciega,
buscando en vano tu alegría
cálida.

Encorvados,
ambos,
hemos golpeado nuestro sueño
blando.

4

Locked in,
alone,
awaiting your clear
arrival.

You've arrived,
hard,
in your eyes there's a heavy
foul mood.

I've looked at you,
blind,
searching in vain for your warm
joy.

Curved,
both of us,
we've beaten our soft
sleep.

5

Boya zan dé nan ku,
boya añin dé nan fon,
mi nan nun vodoun tché sin.

Vodoun tché sin
dé non oka, dé kpon huanñinan tché,
tó añinhonlòmè.

5

Tal vez la noche que se acerca,
tal vez el día que despierta,
podamos beber el agua de mi vodún.

El agua de mi vodún
que ha pasado la noche en vela,
amor mío, por ti.

5

Perhaps on this night that approaches,
perhaps on this day that awakes,
we can drink the water of my *vodun,*

the water of my *vodun*
that has spent the night in vigil,
my love, for you.

6

Ayigba éhé, dé yé sa wlasusu,
wlasusu huuè yé zin bo zin.
Ayigba míton
ayigba tché.

Hwuénu gugu éhé dé yéyisín,
gugu wihlué huuè éñin.
Hwuénuu míton
hwuénuu tché.

6

Esta tierra, tantas veces vendida,
tantas veces aplastada.
Vuestra tierra
y la mía.

Este tiempo inútilmente encadenado,
inútilmente detenido.
Vuestro tiempo
y el mío.

6

This earth, so often sold,
so often flattened.
Your land
and mine.

This time uselessly chained,
uselessly detained.
Your time
and mine.

Ayigba dji huè yé tè
gbètolè sin agbaza yuyu dó
kpodo oku gugu tata,
bò godó sin homè mèdièlètonmè
omyó nun ñinñlan sò tó djidji
bosòtóté tata.
Nun ñinñlan gugu.

Tó hò fifa dé mè
adó dagbédé lilè dó
yé dió nun lèkpo;
gan awédélè sò wa tó nunko,
yé na aló na yé délè.

Evosodjè nun gugu tata dji,
ahwuan gbètolèton,
oku kunontolèton.

Evosèdjè nun gugu tata dji,
Xuvènun …

7

Han quedado sobre la tierra
los oscuros cuerpos de los hombres
de inútil muerte,
y en el oculto corazón de los demás
arde todavía la llama del odio
estúpidamente despierto.
Inútil odio.

En una apacible cobijo
de hermosas paredes
todo ha sido cambiado;
dos hombres importantes se han sonreído,
se han dado la mano.

De nuevo todo inútil,
la lucha de los vivos,
la muerte de los muertos.

De nuevo todo inútil,
el hambre …

7

Above the ground have remained
the dark bodies of the men
of useless deaths,
and in the hidden hearts of the others
the flame of hatred burns still,
stupidly alive.
Useless hate.

In a peaceful shack
with lovely walls
everything has been changed;
two important men have smiled,
they've shaken hands.

Once more all is useless,
the struggle of the living,
the death of the dead.

Once more,
hunger ...

8

N'tó dindin fidé tchintchinmè pèpè té
fidé mè awé non wa
kpé yédé dó;
n'ma só tó dindin nañin n'lokpo
dé na tó sissè juhuii juhuii dó
nan apka tohué.

8

Quisiera descubrir el justo centro
donde se encuentran por fin
las dos personas;
no ser ya más una tendencia sola
acercándose a tientas
a la otra.

8

I wanted to discover the precise centre
where two people
at last meet;
to not be, any longer, one lone inclination
fumblingly approaching
the other.

9

Amlón dé ma din mi zanmè
uuwè sa vó nan
hwuédévonu sin nun flinflin lè.

−Aló tohué, dédòo
watỏ dindin
akissi xóxó dé wayi−

Amlón dé ma din mi zanmè
uuwè wa sunsun
hwuédévonu sin nun flinflin lè.

9

Noches en vela
me traen
recuerdos de otras jornadas.

-Tu mano, dormida
insinúa
una caricia lejana−

Noches en vela
borraron
recuerdos de otras jornadas.

9

Nights in vigil
bring me
memories of other days.

(Your hand, asleep,
insinuates
a distant caress.)

Nights in vigil
erase
memories of other days.

10

Ma kissimi égbé gblo,
asutché.

Ma kissimi gblo
vivè gbètontó dé nabu
tó nuntoémè dó bu nami.

Ma kissimi égbé gblo,
asutché.

Ma kissimi gblo
dé wua sú nunmitonlè
kpodo oku susu gbau.

Ma kissimi égbé gblo,
asutché.

Ma kissimi gblo
ohgi susu gò nun tché
kpo tchidi adulè.

10

No me beses hoy,
esposo.

No me beses
que temo perder en tu boca
tanta humanidad doliente.

No me beses hoy,
esposo.

No me beses
que ha sellado nuestras bocas
tanta muerte.

No me beses hoy,
esposo.

No me beses
que siento llena mi boca
de cuchillos como dientes.

10

Do not kiss me today,
husband.

Do not kiss me
for I fear losing in your mouth
so much painful humanity.

Do not kiss me today,
husband.

Do not kiss me;
so much death
has sealed our mouths.

Do not kiss me today,
husband.

Do not kiss me
for I feel my mouth is full
of knives like teeth.

11

Huanñinan zan mitontó
djè ongbodji.
Mèdélè tin botó amlón dò juhuii
bò yé ma sé.

Ohon wè nunkuntohuélè ñin
Démin n'non mon
Ahjua susu dé yé zin, bo zin
tó anon tché mè.

11

El amor de nuestro lecho
sale a la calle.
Hay quienes duermen tranquilos
y no lo saben.

Tus ojos son las ventanas
en las que encuentro
tantos gritos ahogándose
dentro del pecho.

11

The love of our bed
goes out into the street.
There are those who sleep peacefully
and don't know it.

Your eyes are the windows
in which I find
so many shouts smothering themselves
inside my chest.

12

Tó akpa lokpo kpo awéto kpo
sin oxu sin okin susuton,
ayigba zizè

Tó akpa lokpo kpo awéto kpo
sin oxu sin okin susuton.

> *Zan télème wè*
> *ogbè tché nan si gan nan nun sissin?;*
> *ali kpèvi télème wè*
> *oyè tché na gbon zizoni dó wai dó?;*
> *whué tèlè wè*
> *na wa góo bo nan non zan tchélè mè?*

Tó akpa lokpo kpo awéto kpo
sin oxu sin okin susuton,
huanñinan tché, huanñinan tché.
Tó akpa lokpo kpo awéto kpo
sin oxu sin okin susuton.

12

A una y otra ribera
del mar de arena,
descuartizada.

A una y otra ribera
del mar de arena.

> ¿En qué lechos
> germinará mi vida;
> por qué sendas
> caminará mi sombra;
> qué gemidos
> poblarán mis noches?

A una y otra ribera
del mar de arena,
amado, amado.
A una y otra ribera
del mar de arena.

12

Both shores
of the sea of sand,
fissured.

From one shore to the other
of the sea of sand.

> In what beds
> will my life germinate;
> down which paths
> will my shadow walk;
> what groans
> will populate my nights?

From one shore to the other
of the sea of sand,
beloved, beloved.
From one shore to the other
of the sea of sand.

13

Huanñinan huè yé non yoluèdó, huanñinan.
Amon yé man ñuè dò
esò n'ganñin ahwangbigblé
bò esoñi ahwanfunfun.

Huanñinan huè yé non yoluèdó, huanñinan.
Amon é non wuadjò
é non wua hen tó akonnu étonmè
oku lèkpo kpatakpata.

Huanñinan huè yé non yoluèdó, huanñinan.
Amon é na wuua ó
bò kèn éton sin nunsissè
na wua hu yé é ó.

13

Amor le llaman, amor.
Pero no saben
que puede ser derrota
y es un combate.

Amor le llaman, amor.
Pero sucede
que conserva en su seno
toda la muerte.

Amor le llaman, amor.
Pero vendrá
y el brillo de su odio
les matará.

13

Love they call it, love.
But they don't know
that it can be defeated,
and is a battle.

Love they call it, love.
But it turns out
it guards in its breast
all death.

Love they call it, love.
But it will come
and the gleam of your hate
shall kill them.

14

Fifa dagbé uwè añin
bodó gbon, bléun bléun, gbon sè tchémè

Ogó uéué uwè añin
bodó wa gba
tó alomè nami.

Fifa dagbé uwè añin
bodó yau ñin, nun bubu non.

Dé o sè fatomè din
dó nin dó non
bodó ñon nien.

Sa yau wayi, fifatché
Sa yau wayi.

14

Eres presencia benéfica
que pasó, fugaz, por mi alma.

Eres el frasco blanco
que se ha quebrado
en mis manos.

Eres presencia benéfica
que presurosa, se pierde.

Así lo decidió el destino
para que así sea
y sea bueno.

Pasa ya, presencia mía,
pasa ya.

14

You are a benevolent presence
that passed, fleetingly, through my soul.

You are the white flask
that has shattered
in my hands.

You are the benevolent presence
quickly lost.

That's what fate has decided,
that it shall be so
and it shall be good.

Pass now, my presence,
pass now.

15

Din ato amlon dò.
Bo, to zinflu sin adlro tohué lè mè,
boya abè wuè éñi.

Din ato amlon dò.
Bo, to zinflu sin adlró tohué lè mè,
boya huuun wuè yéñi.

Din ato amlon dò.
Bo, to zinflu sin adlró tohué lè mè,
Boya axua wuè é ñin.

Yaa.., yaau fon!
bò ni dlró tohué lè wua djè min
anan wa món mi.

15

Ahora duermes.
Y en tus sueños oscuros,
tal vez silencio.

Ahora duermes.
Y en tus sueños oscuros,
tal vez murmullos.

Ahora duermes.
y en tus sueños oscuros,
tal vez el grito.

¡Despierta ya!
y al desnudar tus sueños
me encontrarás.

15

Now you sleep.
And in your dark dreams,
perhaps silence.

Now you sleep.
And in your dark dreams,
perhaps murmurs.

Now you sleep.
And in your dark dreams,
perhaps the shout.

Wake now!
And on undressing your dreams,
you'll find me.

16

Un'na wa sisè dèdè ohjón nunhuiiton
(odè énin dé non wuayikpé
–azan godó azan–
nun yiyló gandjan gandjan
nunkun tché lè ton).

Un'na wa sisè dèdè ohjón nunhuiiton:
étè wè huanñinan tchélè sin alò sisa nan ñin,
bodó ñin nun kuku dé gbon agbaza
nun flinflin jójó tohué dji?

16

Empujaré despacio la puerta del silencio
(esa oración que acude
–día tras día–
al reclamo angustioso
de mis ojos).

Empujaré despacio la puerta del silencio:
¿qué será de mis caricias,
yertas ya en la piel de los recuerdos?

16

I shall slowly push the door of silence
                         (that prayer that heeds
                         – day after day –
            the oppressive call
                         of my eyes).

I shall slowly push the door of silence:
                  what shall become of my caresses,
                  inert now on the skin of memories?

17

Agahomè dé non kpé ayigbalè kpodi aslolè
… n'dé kpékpé matin to asiko dé wayilè
é na wa non djikunmè
bo boya o myón dé tun ogan
sin nun flinflin gbigblólè
alò délèton dé ma do nunkunkpikpon.

17

¡Horizontes como nubes!
… nada en el pasado
habitará la lluvia
y tal vez la llama forje
tibios recuerdos
de unas manos ciegas.

17

Horizons like clouds!
... nothing in the past
shall inhabit the rain
and perhaps the flame forges
lukewarm memories
of blind hands.

18

Oyè nien n'ñin nien mon,
amon fifavivi kpèvi ma tin
bò tó onunflòlèmè djehon yovotonlè
non tó yé dé kplé.
Oyè nien n'ñin nien mon
ekpo kouun kouun na do ñin axjua.

18

Soy sombra pues,
pero no hay brisa
y en los labios se acumulan
los inviernos.
Soy sombra pues
A flor de grito.

18

I am shadow then,
but there is no breeze
and on my lips the winters
accumulate.
I am shadow then
about to shout.

19

Otò gbamè matin nan adlrolè
dé non fa nun gbigla zanmè tchélèton:
yé non chyan lokpo lokpo nunvivè onuvo osindooton
Axjualó ni gbò djèñon namiló!
… nan avilè ni wa dio édélè do ofinlè dji
bona do yí kpodó honhlon ohjuun dé nan ogbè
tò nou dé djè vò afinon bodó to obu donami

Ozan tó fifon to là odékanmèton.

19

No hay aluvión para los sueños
que humedecen mis noches desoladas:
uno a uno eligen el dolor del sumidero.
¡Séame pues propicio el grito!
… y que las lágrimas se vuelvan zarpas
para arrancar una sangre fértil
del vacío gris que me atenaza.

Amanece más allá del palmeral.

19

There is no stream for the dreams
that moisten my desolate nights:
one by one they choose the ache of the drain.
Let the scream, then, be mine!
… and let tears turn into claws
to tear away fertile blood
from the grey void that grips me.

Sunrise beyond the palm grove.

20

Guigon tohué,
di nudjè vò dé to ahí dja
bo non djè agbagba nan
nunkpinkponlè dé madó ta.

Nun lèkpo nonté.

Guigon tohué:
záan fifiènon énin dé wua didon yi
tó fidé n'tó té non kpon
zinguindin fifón non sin nun yòyò dé
dé nan tò didó nami dò a wa.

Guigon tohué,
wua zé mi dòamlon,
wua zé mi dókudlró .

N'toli n'to sisé gbigbò sisien odjlèton
dé non gbon akonnun tché kpodo zaaan..lè démin
dé hjon yí son akpa tché
–son akpa tohué–
kpodo zaaan..lè dé non hwla iédélè
bo yé non gbigbè nan dó kpon mi.

Guingon tohué
wua zé mi dòamlon,
wua zé mi dókudlró.

20

Tu ausencia,
como un vacío que se cae
y desnuda las miradas
de sentido.

Todo detenido

Tu ausencia:
el doloroso instante prolongado
donde espero
el despertar ruidoso de algo nuevo
anunciando que has llegado.

Tu ausencia
me ha dormido,
me ha soñado.

Porque siento el tenso respirar del tiempo
cruzarme el pecho con segundos que se escapan
de mi lado
–de tu lado–
con segundos que se esconden
y se niegan a mirarnos.

Tu ausencia
me ha dormido,
me ha soñado.

20

Your absence,
like an emptiness that falls
and undresses
the meaningful gazes.

Everything halted.

Your absence:
the painful prolonged moment
in which I await
the noisy awakening of something new,
announcing that you have arrived.

Your absence
has lulled me to sleep,
has dreamed me.

Because I feel time's tense breathing
crossing my breast with seconds that escape
from my side
(from your side)
with seconds that hide
and refuse to look at us.

Your absence
has lulled me to sleep,
has dreamed me.

21

I

Nami dindin to làalè
dé tò yé délè su.
Nami non gbà aliólè
dé mon non djèbibè dji.
Nami non tó didlèn alòlè
dé non klen afò
kpodo vitri nunkundélè ton
dé ma dó homè wunwun.

> *−Bo é konu*
> *wuédélènu,*
> *nàn osundé*
> *sin huémannon−.*

I

Nami busca en horizontes
que se cierran.
Nami construye caminos
que no empiezan.
Nami tendiendo las manos
que tropiezan
con el cristal de unos ojos
sin tristeza.

> –Y rie,
> algunas veces,
> a una luna
> de papeles–.

21

I

Nami searches in horizons
that close.
Nami builds paths
that do not begin.
Nami extending hands
that stumble
against the glass of eyes
without sadness.

(And laughs,
sometimes,
at the paper
moon.)

II

Nunkiko ahublanunton:
Numi mu ñin Numi
dé dó nunkunmè ohónonton
sin hwuèmandjò ton lèkpo,
sin wiwonmèton ton lèkpo.

Ékpodo mè dé man dibu nan vidjidji xó!

Ahjua dé yé su do ta nan:
Nami sòvò gò wa ñin Nami.
Edó to nunkununlèmè nun tata,
dé wa xuxu nun kpikpon éton
ayí avivònon kplankplanlè.

Ékpodo mè dé madji oyá kpon!

II

Risa triste:
Nami no es Nami
que tiene el rostro preñado
de todas las injusticias,
de todos los olvidados.

¡Ay de quién no tema el parto!

Grito encerrado:
Nami vuelve a ser Nami.
Tiene los ojos vacíos,
que han secado su mirada
tantos corazones fríos.

¡Ay de quien no haya sufrido!

II

Sad laughter:
Nami is not Nami
whose face is impregnated
with all injustices,
with all the forgotten.

　　　¡Ay! for those who don't fear childbirth!

Confined shout:
Nami becomes Nami once more.
She has empty eyes,
for so many cold hearts
have dried her gaze.

　　　¡Ay! for those who have not suffered!

Ayòlè dé djè min
nan Nami
(dé man sò tó Nami ñin wuè)
ni sòvò gò wua ñin Nami.

> *−Bo ékonu,*
> *wuédélènu,*
> *nán osundé*
> *sin huémannon−.*

Ayòlè dé lilè dó yé dé.
agbaza étondé hun myò
non wa gò, zan godó zan godó,
nun tata awua délèton.

Ayòlè dé o fon
Wiwua mè yéton
nun ñin ñlanlè kpo kpata,
yé yi dó kun éton dò zanlòdji.

> *−Bó, yé gba*
> *wuédélènu,*
> *osun ahublanon*
> *sin huémannon−.*

III

Sexos desnudos
que Nami
(no siendo Nami)
vuelve a ser Nami.

        –Y ríe,
        algunas veces,
        a una luna
        de papeles–.

Sexos volcados.
Su cuerpo cálido
puebla, noche tras noche,
el vacío de unos brazos.

Sexos despiertos.
Llegan
todos los horrores,
siembran el lecho.

        –Y rompen,
        algunas veces,
        la luna triste
        de papeles–.

III

Undressed sexes
that Nami
(not being Nami)
becomes Nami once more.

       (And laughs,
       sometimes,
       at the paper
       moon.)

Overturned sexes.
Her warm body
populates, night after night,
the emptiness of some arms.

Awakened sexes.
All the horrors
arrive;
they sow the bed.

       (And break,
       sometimes,
       the sad paper
       moon.)

IV

Ayòlè dé djè min,
ayòlè dé o fon,
ayòlè dé lilè dó yé dé
bó sò zè ogbè lokpo dó yi,
jhuèkpo ema sò hua nunnien,
to alòlèmin.

Nunkiko ahublanunton,
ahjua dé yé su do tanan

Ékpodo mè dé man dibu nan vidjidji xó!

IV

Sexos desnudos,
sexos despiertos,
sexos volcados
y una vida que se lleva,
sin hacerla,
entre las manos.

Risa triste,
grito encerrado.

¡Ay de quién no tema el parto!

IV

Undressed sexes,
awakened sexes,
overturned sexes
and a life that is carried,
unlived,
in one's hands.

Sad laughter,
confined shout.

  ¡Ay! for those who don't fear childbirth!

22

Echikpodi
adó to nunkuntoémè
yinvi awué.

Yinvi awué kpèvi kòun kòun
to oxhu yuyu démè;
dò nami, djè détó kpikpon mi,
ni yéto tché léemè.

Huédélènu
yé non kan adu dó agbaza tché
yinvi tohuélè.

Yé non duwuédu to kodonunlòdji
énon kpo kpèdé nan osin nin dó yi yé
hwénu oxhu nunkun tohuélèton
non wató guígò kon.

22

Parece
que en los ojos tienes
dos alfileres.

Dos alfileres pequeños
en un mar negro;
dime, tu que me miras,
si yo lo tengo.

A veces
muerden mi cuerpo
tus alfileres.

Bailan sobre la almohada
casi ahogados
cuando el mar de tus ojos
se ha desbordado.

22

It seems
that in your eyes you have
two needles.

Two small needles
in a black sea;
tell me, you who gaze at me,
whether I, too, have them.

Sometimes
your needles
bite my flesh.

They dance upon the pillow
almost drowned
when the sea of your eyes
has overflowed.

23

Afonnun sin afonnun mè:
zàan to fifon, égbò bó djò, alió enin
bò édji ahubla sin kiklé.

Afonnun sin afonnun mè:
owhué dé tchitchè trlon wua sò ñin avivinun.

23

Mañana en la mañana:
amanece, por fin, ese sendero
y nace la luz de la tristeza.

Mañana en la mañana:
el sol reciente se hace lágrimas.

23

Tomorrow in the morning:
that path, at last, dawns
and the light of sadness is born.

Tomorrow in the morning:
the recent sun becomes tears.

Glasi añin tó din,
glasi añin:
amon sisa ojuhuntonlò tó wuézundó
gbon gblè gblè sin tòsisa sin aliólè.

Glasi awua ñin hwuélonu,
glasi awua ñin
bo yèyi dó gbon ojhun kan énin léeme
dó zin yédélè do ayigbamè.

Glasi anan wuañin gudovò,
nungbó, glasi anan wuañi
amon anonlè nan wua flon myón do yédé
to nunfifiè sisió dabgé ojhuntonnon.

Sin kéun kéun ahué tcho wuè na gbon otòlomè
sin keun keun ahué tcho.
Bo yé nan wuañin okun tiiun tiiun
dé nan wua ta tó glasilòmè
gbigbò, nunfifa, olan ton.

Sisió dagbé zàaandéton
—añin, awua ñin, anan wuañin—
fidé nunlèkpo non kpé yédé dó.
Bo ayigba nanvò sò nun
ahan vivi sin nunvivè ogbèton.

24

Eres hielo ahora,
eres hielo:
pero corre el arroyo de la sangre
por recatados cauces.

Fuiste hielo entonces,
fuiste hielo
y la calidez recorrió esas venas
que se hundían en la tierra.

Serás hielo más tarde,
sí, serás hielo
pero se inflamarán los pechos
en el hervor estremecido de la sangre.

Sólo dos gotas recorrerán el río
sólo dos gotas.
Y serán la mínima simiente
que encenderá en el hielo
el palpitar, calmo, de la carne.

El estremecido instante
—eres, fuiste, serás—
donde todo confluye.
Y la tierra beberá de nuevo
el licor acerbo de la vida.

24

You are ice now,
you are ice;
but the surge of blood flows
through concealed channels.

You were ice then,
you were ice;
and the warmth travelled those veins
that sank into the earth.

You shall be ice later,
yes, you shall be ice;
but your breasts shall inflame
in the shivering boiling of blood.

Only two drops shall travel the river,
only two drops.
And they shall be the tiniest seed
that ignites in the light
the beating, calm, of the flesh.

The shivering moment
(you are, you were, you shall be)
where everything comes together.
And the earth shall drink once more
the bitter liqueur of life.

25

Ogó énin dé to aman mun mè,
ogó enin dé dindin
—tata, tata—
alió dé nan djrè fidé zoninzinzon tchélè nan gbon.

Amon ehéo, e man ñin afotchélè
ogó énin
e mon non búdó nan gbigbò tché
afò gudó gudó
Amon ehéo, e man ñin tòsisa sin zonnu
alió enin.

Enontó chichò o sè tché,
kòxuxu tomèdayisunon dé nontó sisèkpo,
yisénon,
dó nan ogó fèsininnon.

Kòxuxu énin dé mon non fóo!
kpódo vivi ayigbanonton!

25

Ese cristal entre las hojas verdes,
Ese cristal buscando
-en balde, en balde-
el camino que encauce mis pasos.

Pero no, no son mis pies
ese cristal
ni lo empaña mi aliento
paso a paso.
Pero no, no es un cauce
ese sendero.

Merodea mi alma,
sedienta vagabunda que se acerca,
ingenua,
al cristal azul.

¡Esa sed de infinito
y el sabor de la tierra!

25

That crystal among the green leaves,
that crystal searching
(in vain, in vain)
for the path my steps take.

But no, they are not my feet,
that crystal,
nor does my breath fog it,
step by step.
But no, it is not a channel,
that path.

My soul prowls,
thirsty vagabond that approaches,
naively,
the blue glass.

That infinite thirst
and the taste of the earth!

26

Nunkikó tohué to okumè, dévohuè eñia?
nundidóton dé non hua buyí
alòlili tohuélèton,
onunflò éninlè dé gò kpodo awadjidjè kaka sò dó yi,
ogbè ma non sò to yémè din, amom ye ma fa ...

Nunkikó tohué to okumè
> *dhayí ohon wuè eñi*
>> *dhayí ana wuè eñin*
>>> *dhayí ogbè wuè eñin.*

26

¿Tu sonrisa en la muerte, era otra?
La insinuada disolución
de tus caricias,
esos labios de eterna alegría,
inmóviles ya, pero no fríos ...

Tu sonrisa en la muerte
> era puerta
>> era puente
>>> era vida.

26

Your smile in death, was it something else?
The insinuated dissolution
of your caresses,
those lips of everlasting joy,
now still, but not cold …

Your smile in death
                was door
                        was bridge
                                was life.

27

I

Nungblágodó dé avunlè hjua adó dó
hu jun mitonlè;
wan ñinñlanlè to aga hi
—yé gò huédjahilò—.

Bo lèblanun enin dé ma dé nin ku
kuxhuéton; abè enin
dé mlan okunon hjan;
oho gugu eninlè
non tèdó jein vegomè,
non fluflu nukiken nunkuntonlè,
non doténan alòlè.

> *—Odjé ohjun miton*
> *sò gbé sò*
> *vivò ohjunton!—*

27

I

Esquinas orinadas por los perros
asesinan nuestra sangre;
suben sórdidos hedores
—llenan la tarde —.

Y esta tristeza impotente
de cementerio; este silencio
que canta himnos de muerte;
estas palabras inútiles
se agarran a la garganta,
embotan el brillo de los ojos,
ponen frenos a las manos.

> —¡Ay, nuestra sangre
> cada día
> menos sangre!—

27

I

Street corners marked by dogs
murder our blood;
sordid stenches rise
(they fill the afternoon).

And the impotent sadness
of the cemetery; this silence
that sings hymns of death,
these useless words
clutch the throat,
dull the eyes' shine,
block the hands.

(¡Ay! our blood,
every day
is less blood!)

II

Kòfunfun afifinon aliolèton
hu ojhun miton
bò n'sé gbigbò fifa eton
to akpa huédjahi lonon.

Nun yisénon osòsisá
eninton kpenmi,
nunkun dé yé du dé dji nonvè,
alò eninlè dé yé dó kan nun nan
bodó nan yau ñin tchélè,
fiò mion dó nan nun kuku
axjualè dé yé yi do akluzu dji.

> *−Odjé ohjun miton*
> *asutché,*
> *odjé ohjun miton!−*

II

El polvo gris de las calles
asesinan nuestra sangre
y escucho su latir frío
a la orilla de la tarde.

Me pesa el aire sumiso
de aquel caballo castrado,
duelen los ojos vencidos,
aquellos brazos esclavos
que pronto serán los míos,
queman las muertas figuras
de gritos crucificados.

> −¡Ay nuestra sangre,
> esposo!
> ¡Ay nuestra sangre!−

II

The grey dust of the streets
murders our blood
and I hear its cold beating
on the shore of the afternoon.

I'm troubled by the submissive air
of that gelding,
those conquered eyes ache,
and those enslaved arms
that soon shall be mine,
the dead figures
of crucified shouts, burn.

> (¡*Ay!* our blood,
> husband,
> ¡*ay!* our blood!)

28

Egbé nungblágodó xó akpa nan nunkuntchélè
bò akónnú gba hun dó nan guiguon xogan dévolèton.

N'ñuein, n'ñuein;
to okpa diè okintò
wooó ka o tó ñyinñyin
bò n'din, to dlròlèmè,
nunkiken dé non xó o tò.
Amon aliolè yi kpouun
wan ñinñlan yéton.

N'ñuein, n'ñuein;
to okpa diè okintò
wooó ka o tó ñyinñyin
bò afotchélè man gan tron sin
aganlè dé non dó akpa nan mè,
tó fifa nungblágodólèton
alio eninlèton.

28

Hoy hieren mis ojos las esquinas
y palpitan en mi pecho ausencias de otros sones.

Lo sé, lo sé;
al otro lado de la arena
sopla ya el harmatán
y he buscado, en sueños,
los brillos que erizan la laguna.
Pero las calles sólo canalizan
los hedores.

Lo sé, lo sé;
al otro lado de la arena
sopla ya el harmatán
y tengo los pies anclados
en las hirientes piedras,
en las frías esquinas
de estas calles.

28

Today the corners wound my eyes
and the absences of other sounds beat in my chest.

I know, I know;
on the other side of the sand
the Harmattan is already blowing
and I have sought, in dreams,
for the glimmers the lake emits.
But the streets only channel
the stenches.

I know, I know;
on the other side of the sand
the Harmattan is already blowing
and my feet are anchored
in the wounding stones,
on the cold corners
of these streets.

29

Kléklé akónnú hunhunlèton djahi.
Nun danu wiwa lè yèhwésin ohjunton enin!

29

Cae la luz de abiertos pechos.
¡Ese cruel bautismo de la sangre!

29

Light falls from open chests.
That cruel baptism of blood!

30

Zan kpodo kléké kpo
to gbigbon ohunkan iétonlèmè
bò tó nun wiwa iétonlèmè
owuédudu djò.

Un'wa hiai, lokpo lokpo, aliòvi étonlè
din tó lá eton,
n'to sisèkpo agbazafunfun étonton
bò un'wa mon tó nunkunun étonlèmè
nunkpikpon énin.

Owuédudu djò, einh,
owuédudu djò.

Un'wa mon dé o tó awué
wuató titrlon son yémè.
Zoninzizon éninlè ñin dái uéué
Gbèviyiya iétonlèkpo ñin dái yuyu,
Ohó éninlè.

Owuédudu djò, einh,
owuédudu djò.

Din n'nò zédéé do akonnon iétonlèmè,
okun yòyò,
kpodo ohjué tó akpa lokpo
kpodo nunwiwlwn zinfluflú
atinmanmèton do dó non kplé ñindé.

Owuédudu djò, einh,
owuédudu djò.

Meènun wuè nan doténan oxju éninlè?
meènun wuè nan dohún nan djohoón énin?

Ekako ñin nun kòñinkpò guégué
dé zété do nan agbaza miton éninlè,
bódó gbon hunkan miton lèkpo kpata
zanlè kpodo kléklélè.

Bò yé ñin owuédudu, einh,
yé ñin owuédudu.

30

Corren por sus venas
la noche y la mañana
y en todos sus gestos
nace la danza.

Conté, uno a uno, sus dedos
lejos ahora,
me acerco a su piel de espuma
y vi nacer en sus ojos
esa mirada.

Nace la danza, sí,
nace la danza.

Vi luego como brotaban
en ellos dos continentes.
Eran blancos aquellos pasos
eran negras todas sus quejas,
esas palabras.

Nace la danza, sí,
nace la danza.

Me acojo ahora en sus brazos,
los nuevos brotes,
con el sol en un extremo
y olor obscuro en las hojas,
acurrucada.

Nace la danza, sí,
nace la danza.

¿Quién detendrá esos ríos?
¿Quién canalizará ese viento?

Es ya un inmenso caudal
que levantan esos cuerpos,
por todas sus venas corren
las noches y las mañanas.

Y son una danza, sí,
son una danza.

30

Through their veins flow
night and morning,
and in all their gestures
the dance is born.

I counted, one by one, their fingers;
now far away,
I approached their skin of foam
and I saw that look
ignite in their eyes.

The dance is born, yes,
the dance is born.

I then saw how, in them,
two continents sprouted.
Their steps were white,
all their complaints were black,
those words.

The dance is born, yes,
the dance is born.

I now take refuge in their arms,
the new shoots,
with the sun at one extreme
and dark scent in these leaves,
I curl around.

The dance is born, yes,
the dance is born.

Who will stop those rivers?
Who will channel that wind?

It is already an enormous flow
that lifts those bodies,
through all their veins flow
the nights and the mornings.

And they are a dance, yes,
they are a dance.

OMEGA

N'to bu di nan gbélokpo dé mi nan zé midé dò
huablanunmè djikun djidja huedjahi lokpoton
bo ogbè mitonlè, fifamè tonnon dé oñin
nan avivi tègbètegbènu bodé du yé dé dji,
man nan mon gbédé
hlonhlon dé mi dó egbé bodó zehi do aga
kpodo ya djidji kpo,
boka non sò wa din tègbè zanfifon yòyò lokpo,
nan ni do djè tron sò oho lokpo,
boya nunkiken lokpoton.

> −Nun kpédé tègbè,
> nunvòvò gbédé−.

Huablanunmè djikun djidja huédjahi lokpoton
dé non gò, uédélènun, nunkuntoélè;
dé non vò kòn, uédélènun, trlon o nun tohué
kpodo tché osu.

Huablanunmè djikun djidja huédjahi lokpoton
non sin hun miton
kpodo vivè −amlònnun−
sin kan dé man do nunkunukpon kpo drlòkuku.

Huablanunmè djikun djidja huédjahi lokpoton
démè mi wayo nan taglomè mitonlè
kpodo hun mitonlè.
EHEO.

Minitchité lokpo dógò …,
n'toli nunkun dévolè to dindin ohjué détò huixwla édé.
Alò devolè to tintenkpon nan gbin
akpòkpò dé txion ehé.

To hun dévolèmè
amlonsisa dé dú dó dji.
EHEO.
Agbò kpémi, huañinantché …, obu dimi.

OMEGA

Temo que algún día nos hundamos
en la tristeza de una tarde lluviosa
y nuestras vidas, húmedas ya para siempre
de lágrimas cotidianas y vencidas,
no encuentren jamás
las fuerzas con que hoy las levantamos
penosamente,
constantes en la busca de un amanecer nuevo,
recreado a partir de una palabra,
quizá un brillo.

> –Siempre poca cosa,
> nunca nada–.

La tristeza de una tarde lluviosa
que invade, a veces, tus ojos;
que rebosa, a veces, de tu boca
y de la mía.

La tristeza de una tarde lluviosa
que nos ata el corazón
con penosos –adormecedores–
lazos de desesperanza y de sueño.

La tristeza de una tarde lluviosa
en la que masturbábamos nuestros cerebros
y nuestros corazones.
NO.

Levantémonos de nuevo …,
hay otros ojos en busca del oculto sol.
Otras manos intentan arrancar
las nubes que lo cubren.

En otros corazones
el sopor ha sido vencido.
NO.
Estoy cansada, amor …, y tengo miedo.

OMEGA

I am afraid that one day we might sink
into the sadness of a rainy afternoon
and our lives, now forever damp
from defeated and daily tears,
might never find
the strength with which we lift them today,
sadly,
steadfast in the search for a new dawn,
recreated from a word,
perhaps a sparkle.

        (Always a small thing,
        never nothing.)

The sadness of a rainy afternoon
that sometimes invades your eyes
and sometimes spills from your mouth
and from my own.

The sadness of a rainy afternoon
that binds our hearts
with sad (lulling)
ties of hopelessness and sleepiness.

The sadness of a rainy afternoon
on which we masturbated our minds
and our hearts.
NO.

Let us rise up again …
there are other eyes in search of the hidden sun.
Other hands try to tear away
the clouds that cover it.

In other hearts
the weariness has been defeated.
NO.
I am tired, my love … and I am afraid.

Glossary

Adjarrá	Town near Porto-Novo where an important weekly market is held.
Adjogán	Dance performed by the princesses of Hogbonu (see below) for their king.
Agóo	Interjection used to open a path in a crowd. ("Make way!" "Careful!")
Ahwangbó	*Lit.* "The War Is Over": Market built in 1945 to commemorate the end of the Second World War.
Evivi	Exclamation indicating pleasure, joy or satisfaction.
Heviosó	One of the main *voduns* of the Dahomean pantheon. The representation of thunder and lightning. Heviosó corresponds to Changó in the Yoruban tradition.
Hogbonu	*Lit.* "Beside the Great House": the traditional name of the city now known as Porto-Novo, Benin.
Kpèsè	An almost ritual voice that incites calm.
Ñeñe	Affectionate nickname, diminutive of "Agnès" made by removing the first and last letter and repeating it twice (*Gnè-Gnè* in French, *Ñeñe* in Spanish).
Sèmè-Kpodji	Town in southeastern Benin.
Sodabi	Palm brandy.
Vodun	Sacred representation of natural forces, animals or ancestors in a pantheist conception of the universe. The *voduns* correspond to the *orishas* of the Yoruban tradition.
Yohô	Family altar, at which tribute is paid to ancestors.